FAMILY FOR LIFE

MARLENE SOTO

FOREWORD

We are born into this world and guided by our parents. After becoming a Mom I learned as parents we serve as the port where our children pull up to the dock when they need to be filled up and then continue on their life journey. Parenting is a journey no matter how many people you talk to, how many videos you watch nothing can prepare you for your own personal experience because everyones life is different. We all have different traumas, different life experiences, and different children that will separate how you personally receive parenthood. One thing is for sure regardless, this roundtrip ticket to life must be lived and parenthood reminds you of the smallest joys in life because you watch life start from the beginning again. However, sometimes it becomes hard to just live because everyday you are giving all you've got to your children and family and in the end you're on empty for yourself. So who fills your cup? For some our own parents have transitioned, or some have an estranged relationship with them or some just don't want their parents to know they are going through something. As we get older we try and protect our parents because they are getting older and we realize all the sacrifices they made and want them in peace. Either way that cup needs to be filled. That may mean a night out with your friends, a vent session on the phone, a hobby that allows you to release all the pain, or maybe just a good book that is relatable and makes you feel like you're not alone in this journey. Marlene has been gifted with a grace and nurturing energy that makes you feel seen. She has been very transparent in her experience as a Mother to a special needs child. Through the highs, the lows and everything in between one thing that stays the same with Marlene and that is her will to fight for her children to make sure they feel heard and seen. She has taken the plot twist in her journey of motherhood and has created a movement that will revolutionize how we view special needs children. She is opening the doors of difficult conversions and its creating an awareness for the true reality of what these parents endure day to day. Allowing us to have grace with ourselves and others mothers. To not judge but lend a hand, a voice or just an ear. We never know why we are chosen for certain experiences in life but either way we must find the joy within it because in the end no matter what there is an unexplained love and joy with becoming a Mother, and Marlene is the MVP in this game. May your cup be filled and may you feel seen as she brings you into her world.

-Jenn Pinto

Boom! One minute you are living life and the next you are responsible for one. Now let's get a few things straight and out of the way so that you can understand who I am. My name is Marlene. I am a wife, daughter, sister and the most important role I have is a mom. I am writing from a professional perspective and personal experiences. Professionally I have worked alongside doctors, therapists, educators and more. My personal experiences ranged from being a caregiver to my father, a mom to a special needs child and taking care of myself.

Being responsible for the care of a loved one is an honor but it is also draining. I am here to speak my truth on how rocky the emotions get while nursing or caring for your loved ones can be. We will go through the good, bad and ugly then back to the good. I will share my heartfelt moments, give advice and simply vent. Remember there is no rule book to life, parenthood and the caregiver role. Along the way you will find some positive affirmations, quotes and suggested activities to keep you on the path that was chosen for you. Sit back, get cozy and let's begin.

One minute you are living your life and the next you are responsible for one. What does this really mean? Well depending on what your life looked like before the change, it will vary person to person. You can be happily married trying to conceive or be the complete opposite single pregnant without even trying. During the pregnancy if you are told that there is a possibility that your child would be born with a disability that gives you time to mentally prepare for what the future may hold. If you're like me I had no time to prepare immediately after delivering my son. He was whisked away to the Neonatal Intensive Care Unit. It was at that very moment I realized my son would be disabled and need 24 hour care. One day at a time was the new motto someone told me to live by. It was exactly what I did when you are at the hospital's mercy you can only focus on that minute that hour that day. Keep this thought in mind we will revisit children born with a life long condition later on.

ne minute you are living your life and the next you are responsible for one. What can this mean? Picture yourself in your best years, career driven finally settled in your own home. Traveling and fine dining are your hobbies. Suddenly one of your parents gets sick, injured or worse they are terminally ill. What now ? How do you alter your entire life that you just became acclimated too and become a caregiver? Do you have other siblings to share these responsibilities with or are you an only child? If you do have other siblings, which of you will be the responsible one? The truth is every situation may vary. You may all be responsible but there will always be the one person who takes more on than the others. Most people will be there without any hesitation for their parents day in day out. Putting themselves, their love lives, their social lives and even their career on hold to be supportive.

One minute you are living your life and the next you are responsible for one. Every scenario is different. Now let's say you meet the love of your life, you are head over heels for one another, you are swept off your feet. You decide to take it to another level and commit monogamously to one another. For some that may look like marriage, for others that can be the verbal vow to commit. Now picture this happy relationship that feels like a honeymoon everyday and you get the phone call that no one wants to receive. Your partner is in an accident that leaves them disabled for life. Your partner whom you love to go out, dance with and make love to now can't do any of those things without your assistance. How do you feel about spending the rest of your life caring for someone everyday all day? Now this relationship example sounds like a dream or a movie but we all know that there is no such thing as a perfect relationship. Yes you can be happy in love and even best friends with your partner but this accident will put a strain on your relationship. How tight is your bond, how strong is that commitment you made? How about a relationship on the rocks barely holding on what happens now? Do you stay with them out of pity and empathize with your partner? Do you leave because your relationship was hard enough before the accident and you know you cannot sustain this trauma? A Lot of questions, many decisions in so little time.

All of these scenarios go from one extreme to the next. These accidents, diseases, and births occur very frequently. There is a great chance that you will fall into one of these categories in your lifetime. Even after knowing this you will not be prepared for that moment. Nothing can prepare you for this moment. Most people will go through multiple stages of emotions. In no particular order you can blame yourself, question why this would happen, feel helpless, over do it and even live in denial. In the end most people will be the supportive love one, parent intuition will kick in and you will learn how to process the change. The next few pages I will share some positive affirmations that you can say, repeat and share. These words of positivity definitely helped me through some of my darkest days.

I was chosen to be great

I was hand picked to be a nurturer

My destiny has been set before me

Accept and adapt to all changes

Grace and Favor is over me

I can handle whatever is set before me

I am a better person because of the challenges
I was presented with

Not all Heroes wear capes

I have many callings and this is one of them

This journey will be another part of my testimony

Having the title of parent is truly an honor. The idea of raising a child whether planned or unplanned birthed or adopted is such a beautiful experience over all. Whether it is your first child or fourth child, parenting a child with a disability can be so difficult. Everyone handles the news differently. I personally immersed myself into learning all the facts and statistics, patients personal stories that I could. This is how I chose to cope with the news that my son would be disabled for life. I didn't know at the time that it was coping. I just thought being knowledgeable would be beneficial to my child's future.

Parenthood suddenly means that you are now a 24 hour educator, disciplinary, chef and nurse just to name a few. As much as you enjoy the baby milestones like sitting, walking, talking for the parents of the disabled child we don't have that timeline. Our milestones are so small yet so important. For example my child never laughed or smiled. My son took months to smile and even longer to laugh and when he did we jumped for joy. Over the years your child grows and you prepare them for the real world. You prepare them for the day they move out on their own and actually some of us count those days down. We all know teenage years are hard. Now with a disabled child their future can vary. Some children will grow up to be high functioning and more independent. This independence can mean that their disability will not interfere with living on their own, working a job and experiencing more typical life expectations.

Raising a permanently disabled child they grow up in a world where they are dependent on their parents for every need. They are not able to do the things that other children can do, and this can be heartbreaking for parents who want to give their child the best life possible. We don't have a move out date. When we start to let reality set in we come to the realization that not just our future will turn out very differently than expected but the future we envisioned our child having. My son was only months old and I was told his life expectancy can be early adulthood. That meant he wouldn't go to prom, have a girlfriend, a family, or go to college. All these thoughts race through your mind. Again here comes parent guilt, questioning my new reality and feeling hopeless. As the years pass from my experience you never accept what your child has, you just learn how to cope and live through it.

n my years of parenting a special needs child, being a special needs advocate here is some advice that was shared with me that I recommend you should **NOT** say to someone who is a caregiver or parent to a child with special needs.

"God gives his toughest battles to its strongest soldiers"

This makes me feel like so you're saying I'm strong and deserved this? Or are you saying that you are weak and unable to handle this? I would rather you say "you are so strong, I commend you.

Oh I understand, my friend had a child ......

Now I know your intentions are meant well but no two kids are alike in any medical condition. I would much rather you say, no two kids are alike but my friend's child.....

Have you tried this yet I heard it cures

I have listened to multiple treatment options, some natural routes, some medicated routes and I am open to hearing of new ways to improve the quality of life. Can you cure it? If there was a cure you should be in the medical journals and be recognized for this as well as helping all the people with the same conditions

Don't listen to doctors they just want insurance money

Being Latina this was a very common one for me. "Doctors do and say whatever so long as they are getting paid" words that were frequently expressed to me. So what you are telling me is that my child is not disabled? My child's needs are for insurance fraud and a paycheck is that way you are explaining to me?

Your child looks normal!

This line right here gets me every time. It is 2022 and people still believe a disability has to be obviously physical. I find this to be extremely rude and I am not mistaken who made you the expert in my loved ones disability to know what features, anomalies and characteristics they lack for their disabilities. There is a week in mid October that is set and celebrated to recognize invisible disabilities.

I can't imagine what you are going through

You are absolutely right you can't! That simple, once again no two persons are alike in any condition.

ow remember earlier on I said that we would go through the good the bad the ugly and now it's time we revisit the good. An act of human kindness can be life changing for the recipient and something so minimal for the person doing the act. These gestures can be done out of the goodness of your heart, intuition or accessibility. You can give in many ways to people you have never met before, people you see but do not personally know, acquaintances, friends, family and more. When you give your time, your help, love and dedication to someone it is a daily choice. You and only you will commit to being that support system. In great faith you would go above and beyond doing things you never imagined or trained for. This will come natural to a caretaker even at its toughest moments and weakest points you will find the strength. Remember The words thank you, I appreciate you may never come. This is your reminder that you are appreciated and your actions are speaking louder than any words. I stand with you, beside you you are not alone.

CONNECT WITH MARLENE

www.theswankids.com

www.helpingswans.com

Mediamarlene@gmail.com